SESAME STREET

T0015902

Explore POLAR HABITATS with Ernie

Charlotte Reed

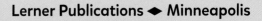
Lerner Publications ◆ Minneapolis

There are many habitats to explore!

In the Sesame Street® Habitats series, young readers will take a tour of eight habitats. Join your friends from *Sesame Street* as they learn about these different habitats where animals live, sleep, and find food and water.

Sincerely,
The Editors at Sesame Workshop

Table of Contents

WHAT IS A HABITAT?

Let's explore habitats! A habitat is a place where animals live, sleep, and find food and water. A polar habitat is a type of habitat.

I'm excited to learn about polar habitats!

Polar habitats are very cold and windy. There is plenty of snow in a polar habitat but usually very little rain. The land is covered in ice and snow!

Elmo loves when it snows on Sesame Street!

LET'S LOOK AT POLAR HABITATS

Even though it's cold, plants can grow in polar habitats. Some polar plants include grasses, lichens, mosses, small shrubs, and flowers.

Flowers grow in my fairy garden too!

There are many kinds of animals that live in polar habitats. Animals in polar habitats find ways to stay warm.

Emperor penguins stay warm by huddling close together in large groups. They take turns being in the middle where it's the warmest.

It's a big, warm hug!

During the coldest months of the year, lemmings burrow under the snow to stay warm. When lemmings burrow, they dig tunnels and build nests for their winter homes.

Snowy owls are covered in thick feathers to protect them from the cold.

They have lots of feathers like my friend Big Bird!

Since it's too cold for trees to grow in polar habitats, snowy owls build their nests on the ground.

Some polar animals have blubber that helps keep them warm. Walruses, harp seals, and beluga whales have blubber.

Polar bears have blubber too.

The musk ox has a thick coat of fur to help keep its body warm. It has hooves that help it dig through the snow to find plants to eat.

Some polar animals, like the Arctic ground squirrel, hibernate. That means they find a safe place and stay there until winter ends.

That's a long time to rest!

Some polar animals, like Arctic foxes, have white fur to help them blend in with the snow and ice. They have long fluffy tails that help keep them warm too.

Their tails wrap around them like blankets!

Polar habitats are very icy, windy, and snowy. They are home to all kinds of animals that find ways to stay warm in the cold.

How do you stay warm when it's cold outside?

CAN YOU GUESS?

1. Which one of these pictures shows a polar habitat?

A

B

2. Which one of these animals lives in a polar habitat?

A

B

Glossary

blubber: the part of whales and other large sea mammals that helps them keep warm

habitat: a place where animals live and can find water, food, and a place to sleep

hibernate: to rest through the winter

huddling: standing very close together to keep warm

Can You Guess? Answers

1. B
2. B

Read More

Huddleston, Emma. *Polar Bears*. Minneapolis: Bearport, 2023.

Peters, Katie. *Polar Animals*. Minneapolis: Lerner Publications, 2020.

Reed, Charlotte. *Explore Mountain Habitats with Big Bird*. Minneapolis: Lerner Publications, 2024.

Photo Acknowledgments

Image credits: Chase Dekker/Wild-Life Images/Getty Images, p. 5; Ruzdi Ekenheim/Getty Images, p. 6; Wu Swee Ong/Getty Images, p. 6 (Reindeer); Mauro Rossi/500px/Getty Images, p. 6 (Snowy owl); troutnut/Getty Images, p. 9; mzphoto11/Getty Images, p. 10; vladsilver/Getty Images, p. 12; Mathilde Poirier/Alamy, p. 14; Dave Hutchison Photography/Getty Images, p. 17; Thomas Kokta/Getty Images, p. 18; alazor/Getty Images, p. 19 (Beluga whale); zanskar/Getty Images, p. 19 (Harp seal); Jami Tarris/Getty Images, p. 19 (Walrus); Karine Patry/Getty Images, p. 20; Nature in Stock/Alamy, p. 23; Cecilie Sønsteby/Getty Images, p. 24; SeppFriedhuber/Getty Images, p. 25; 4FR/Getty Images, p. 26 (Arctic wolves); Global_Pics/Getty Images, p. 26; Karine Patry/Getty Images, p. 27 (Musk ox); ToniFlap/Getty Images, p. 28 (Left); MOF/Getty Images, p. 28 (Right); Jessica Minozzi/500px/Getty Images, p. 29 (Squirrel); Alexey_Seafarer/Getty Images, p. 29 (Polar bear).
Cover: KeithSzafranski/Getty Images, (Emperor Penguins); Ruzdi Ekenheim/Getty Images, (Antartica); Jim Cumming/Shutterstock, (Arctic wolf); Mathilde Poirier/Alamy, (Lemming).

Index

For my grandmother, who always believes in me.

Copyright © 2024 Sesame Workshop®, Sesame Street®, and associated characters, trademarks, and design elements are owned and licensed by Sesame Workshop. All rights reserved.

International copyright secured. No part of this book may be reproduced, stored in a retrieval system, or transmitted in any form or by any means—electronic, mechanical, photocopying, recording, or otherwise—without the prior written permission of Lerner Publishing Group, Inc., except for the inclusion of brief quotations in an acknowledged review.

Lerner Publications Company
An imprint of Lerner Publishing Group, Inc.
241 First Avenue North
Minneapolis, MN 55401 USA

For reading levels and more information, look up this title at www.lernerbooks.com.

Main body text set in Mikado provided by HVD.

Editor: Amber Ross **Designer:** Laura Otto Rinne
Lerner team: Angel Kidd

Library of Congress Cataloging-in-Publication Data

Names: Reed, Charlotte, 1997- author.
Title: Explore Polar habitats with Ernie / Charlotte Reed.
Description: Minneapolis : Lerner Publications, [2024] | Series: Sesame street habitats | Includes bibliographical references and index. | Audience: Ages 4–8 | Audience: Grades K–1 | Summary: "Polar habitats are cold, windy, and snowy. Join Ernie and his Sesame Street friends as they travel to a polar habitat to learn about polar animals and the special features that help them survive"– Provided by publisher.
Identifiers: LCCN 2023004817 (print) | LCCN 2023004818 (ebook) | ISBN 9798765604236 (library binding) | ISBN 9798765617663 (epub)
Subjects: LCSH: Animals—Habitations—Polar regions—Juvenile literature. | Ecology—Polar regions—Juvenile literature. | BISAC: JUVENILE NONFICTION / Science & Nature / Environmental Science & Ecosystems
Classification: LCC QL104 .R44 2024 (print) | LCC QL104 (ebook) | DDC 591.70911—dc23/eng/20230420

LC record available at https://lccn.loc.gov/2023004817
LC ebook record available at https://lccn.loc.gov/2023004818

ISBN 979-8-7656-2489-0 (pbk.)

Manufactured in the United States of America
1-1009560-51410-6/2/2023